LEADERSHIP PRACTICES INVENTORY

LPI

Third Edition

LEADERSHIP DEVELOPMENT PLANNER

JAMES M. KOUZES

BARRY Z. POSNER

Pfeiffer
A Wiley Imprint
www.pfeiffer.com

Published by Pfeiffer
An Imprint of John Wiley & Sons, Inc.
989 Market Street, San Francisco, CA 94103-1741   www.pfeiffer.com

Pfeiffer books and products are available through most bookstores. To contact Pfeiffer directly
call our Customer Care Department within the U.S. at (800) 274-4434, outside the U.S. at
(317) 572-3985 or fax (317) 572-4002.

Pfeiffer also publishes its books in a variety of electronic formats. Some content that appears in print
may not be available in electronic books.

ISBN: 0-7879-6729-7

Acquiring Editor: *Lisa Shannon*
Director of Development: *Kathleen Dolan Davies*
Developmental Editor: *Janis Chan*
Editor: *Rebecca Taff*
Senior Production Editor: *Dawn Kilgore*
Manufacturing Supervisor: *Bill Matherly*
Interior Design: *Yvo*

Printed in the United States of America

Printing   10   9   8   7   6   5   4   3   2   1

CONTENTS

Introduction   Leadership Development is   v
                Self-Development

PART I   CONTINUING YOUR LEADERSHIP DEVELOPMENT

STEP 1   Review the Five Practices   3
STEP 2   Learn How *You* Learn to Lead   7
STEP 3   Review Your Progress and Your Feedback   13
STEP 4   Make New Plans   23
STEP 5   First, Lead Yourself   33

PART II   SELECTING LEADERSHIP DEVELOPMENT RESOURCES

RESOURCE A   Ten Tips for Becoming a Better Leader   37
RESOURCE B   Ways to Improve Your Leadership Practices   47
RESOURCE C   Reading List   79
RESOURCE D   Leadership Development Worksheets   83

ABOUT THE AUTHORS   **89**

Wanting TO LEAD AND believing THAT you *can lead* ARE THE departure POINTS ON THE PATH TO leadership. LEADERSHIP IS AN ART- A *performing* art — AND THE instrument IS THE self.

INTRODUCTION

Leadership Development Is Self-Development

For centuries we've all been living with a pernicious leadership myth. It's the myth that leadership is destiny, reserved for only a few of us. This myth is perpetuated every day, whenever someone asks, "Are leaders born or made?"

Of course all leaders are born. So are all athletes, scholars, artists, accountants, salespeople, and trainers. So what? It's what you do with what you have that's important.

Leadership is not contained in a gene any more, or any less, than other abilities. Leadership is not a place, it's not a position, and it's not a secret code that can't be deciphered by ordinary people. Leadership is an *observable set of skills and abilities.*

Of course, some people are better at leadership than others. Again, so what? The more we attribute leadership to a set of innate character traits, the more we abdicate our own responsibility to become the best we can be. The longer we wait for genetic scientists to help us select the best and the brightest, the longer we avoid personal accountability for the work we now do.

Only by assuming that leadership is a learnable set of practices can we ever discover how many good leaders there really are. Only by assuming that *you* can learn to become a better leader than you are now can you discover your full leadership potential. This is the spirit with which we approach the leadership development process contained in these pages. We *know* that you can learn to be a better leader, and we invite you to continue with us on your lifelong learning journey.

LEADERSHIP DEVELOPMENT IS SELF-DEVELOPMENT

Human beings are toolmakers. We're developers of technology and techniques that enable us to be more productive and more successful at everything we do. Mechanics need tools to repair an engine, artists need brushes to paint a portrait, physicists need computers to perform complex calculations. What, then, are the instruments of a leader?

The leader's primary instrument is the self. That's really all we have to work with. It's not going to be the code written by a brilliant programmer, the smart chip inside the personal digital assistant, or the inspiring script from a clever speechwriter that's going to make us better leaders. It's what we do with our *selves* that makes the difference. The mastery of the art of leadership is the mastery of the self. Leadership development is self-development.

We often ask participants in our leadership workshops to think about a leader from history whom they wish they could have over for dinner and conversation. "If you had this opportunity," we inquire, "what questions would you ask this person?" Invariably, the questions are variations on a few themes: "What made you believe that you could do this?" "What kept you from giving up?" "How did you get the courage to continue?" "What did you do when you were discouraged or afraid?" These are all questions about what was going on inside the person as he or she was experiencing the world. Answering these questions requires a high degree of self-awareness.

The quest for leadership is first and foremost an inner quest to discover who you are. Through self-development comes the confidence needed to lead. Self-confidence is really awareness of and faith in your own powers. These powers become clear and strong only as you work to identify and develop them.

As you work through the pages of this *Leadership Development Planner,* we'll ask you to look within and reveal what you find—if only to yourself. The payoff is great when you do. In our research we've discovered that learning and leading are directly related—the best leaders are also the best learners. When you think about it, it makes complete sense. Those who end up being the best at what they do—be it leading, selling, engineering, accounting, painting, golfing, or playing music—are always eager to learn new skills, techniques, and information. They're curious about themselves and their world. We ask you to bring your own sense of curiosity and eagerness with you as you explore the pages of this Planner.

HOW TO USE THE PLANNER

The *Leadership Development Planner* is designed for leaders who have received feedback using our *Leadership Practices Inventory* (LPI) and have begun a process of acting on that feedback. Research suggests that it takes ten years to develop expertise in something. Leadership is no exception. Becoming a better leader needs to become a habit for the long term. The Planner can help instill that habit.

While the Planner can be used independent of outside assistance, coaching strengthens the likelihood that you will train and practice. We strongly encourage you to seek out someone who can help you stick with the steps in this process, ask you questions about how you're doing, and give you advice and counsel along the way.

During the LPI Workshop, you went through a series of activities to help you understand your LPI feedback, make a short-term improvement plan, take action, meet with a partner to review your progress, and share your LPI feedback with your Observers.

The Planner picks up where the LPI *Participant's Workbook* leaves off. The Planner begins your next phase of leadership development. It is something you can come back to over a period of time and customize to meet your own needs. For example, you might use the Planner:

- In a two-day (or longer) workshop in which you more fully explore options for improving in each of The Five Practices

- In an expert coaching process in which you meet one-on-one every week or two with a leadership specialist

- In a peer coaching process in which you meet once a month or so with others who are also using the Planner to become better leaders

- On your own in preparation for a 90-day to 120-day developmental effort

- As a tool to integrate into your PDA or other day-planner

What's important is that you adopt the same kind of discipline for developing yourself as a leader that you would adopt for improving in any endeavor. You'll get the most out of it, and have the most fun, when you have both the will and the way—the desire and a plan.

WHAT YOU'LL GAIN FROM USING THE PLANNER

As a result of completing the Planner you will be better able to:

- Articulate your ideal image of yourself as a leader

- Discuss how people learn to lead

- Integrate the best leadership learning practices into your own routines

- Consciously review your progress toward becoming a better leader

- Select the kinds of developmental activities that best fit your needs

- Write a plan for the next steps in your leadership development

- Apply an easy-to-use process that can be repeated

WHAT'S IN THE PLANNER

Here's what you'll find in the pages that follow:

- In Step 1, we briefly review The Five Practices of Exemplary Leadership®—the fundamentals of leadership that you learned about in the LPI Workshop and which we discuss at length in our book, *The Leadership Challenge.* In Step 2, we also review the ways in which people learn to lead—or do anything for that matter.

- Step 3 asks you to review the progress you've made so far in becoming a better leader.

- Step 4 walks you through the steps of planning your next developmental actions.

- Step 5 concludes with further observations about where you need to turn to continue your quest to become a better leader.

- Part II provides a collection of more than one hundred ways to become a better leader. These developmental activities are organized around each of The Five Practices and are divided into sections based on the three fundamental ways we learn. When you make your own developmental plans, you can use these activities as options from which to pick and choose what's best for you. You can also use them as idea generators for inventing your own learning projects.

- In addition, we describe the best practices of learning to lead. These best practices are based on our own and others' research, as well as tips from those who've done it—people like yourself who've dedicated themselves to becoming the best leaders they can be.

- Part II also includes a reading list and some blank Leadership Development Worksheets to use in recording your development plans.

THE unique ROLE

OF leaders

IS TO *take us*

TO places

WE'VE **never**

been before.

PART I

Continuing Your Leadership Development

STEP 1

Review the Five Practices

In the LPI Workshop, your facilitator provided an introduction to the research we conducted on leadership and The Five Practices of Exemplary Leadership® that resulted. In this chapter, you will find more details about what we have discovered about exemplary leaders.

We've been conducting intensive research on leadership since 1982. During that entire time, in selecting the people to interview and survey we've consistently chosen not to focus on famous people in positions of power—be they military, political, business, community, or movement leaders—who make headlines. Instead, we've always wanted to know what the vast majority of leaders do—those ordinary people who get extraordinary things done in organizations. We've concentrated our research on people who lead project teams, manage departments, administer schools, organize community groups, and volunteer for student and civic organizations. These folks might be your colleagues at work or your neighbors. They could be *you*. We believe now even more than when we started this work that leadership has absolutely nothing to do with position or status, and everything to do with practice.

In conducting our research we've asked thousands of people, in writing and in interviews, to complete the "Personal-Best Leadership Questionnaire," which we developed to find out what people do day in and day out to mobilize others to want to struggle for shared aspirations. Each person was asked to select a project, program, or significant event that represented a time he or she believed represented his or her own "best practices" leadership experience—the one personally recalled when thinking about a peak leadership performance. Despite the differences in people's individual stories, the Personal-Best Leadership Experiences that we read and listened to revealed similar patterns of action. We found that when leaders are at their personal best, they engage in The Five Practices of Exemplary Leadership®. They:

- Model the Way

- Inspire a Shared Vision

- Challenge the Process

- Enable Others to Act

- Encourage the Heart

In the following paragraphs we've provided brief descriptions of The Five Practices, similar to those you heard during the LPI Workshop. You'll find extensive discussions of each Practice, along with more than one hundred case examples and practical applications in *The Leadership Challenge*.

Model the Way

For more than twenty years we've found in our research that *credibility is the foundation of leadership*. People will not believe the message unless they believe in the messenger. And what is credibility behaviorally? The most frequent response to this question is, "Do what you say you will do" or "DWYSYWD." Embedded in this typical description of credibility are two essentials: *say* and *do*.

Leaders must stand for something, believe in something, and care about something. They must *find their voice* by clarifying their personal values and then express those values in their own style. But good leaders don't force their views on others. Instead, they work tirelessly to build consensus on a set of common principles. Then they *set the example* by aligning their personal actions with shared values. When constituents know that leaders have the courage of their convictions, they become willingly engaged in following that example.

Inspire a Shared Vision

Leaders passionately believe that they can make a difference. They *envision the future* by imagining exciting and ennobling possibilities. But visions seen only by the leader are insufficient to mobilize and energize. Leaders *enlist others* in their dreams by appealing to shared aspirations. They breathe life into ideal and unique images of the future and get people to see how their own dreams can be realized through a common vision.

Challenge the Process

The work of leaders is change. The status quo is unacceptable to them. Leaders *search for opportunities* by seeking innovative ways to change, grow, innovate, and improve. Leaders also *experiment and take risks* by constantly generating small wins and learning from mistakes. Extraordinary things don't get done in huge leaps forward; they get done one step at a time. Leaders demonstrate the courage to continue the quest despite opposition and setbacks.

Enable Others to Act

Leaders know they can't do it alone. Leaders *foster collaboration* by promoting cooperative goals and building trust. Leaders promote a sense of reciprocity and a feeling of "We're all in this together." They understand that mutual respect is what sustains extraordinary efforts. Leaders also *strengthen others* by sharing power and providing choice, making each person feel competent and confident.

Encourage the Heart

The climb to the top is arduous and steep. People become exhausted, frustrated, and disenchanted. They're tempted to give up. Leaders *encourage the heart* of their constituents to carry on. To keep hope and determination alive, leaders *recognize contributions* by showing appreciation for individual excellence. Genuine acts of caring uplift spirits and strengthen courage. In every winning team, the members need to share in the rewards of their efforts, so leaders *celebrate the values and the victories* by creating a spirit of community.

STEP 2

Learn How *You* Learn to Lead

As part of our research, we asked people, "How did you learn to lead?" After we had analyzed thousands of responses, three major learning approaches emerged. We call them the Three E's of learning. In order of frequency of use, they are:

- *Experience:* Learning through trial and error
- *Example:* Learning by observing others
- *Education:* Learning through formal training

Experience: Learning Through Trial and Error

There's no substitute for learning by doing. Learning from trial and error—that "school of hard knocks" people talk about so often—is not just a saying. More people mentioned experience as the most important way to learn to lead than mentioned any other approach. Experience was mentioned almost twice as often as example and nearly three times as often as education. The more chances you have to actually practice leading in real-life situations, the more likely it is that you'll become a better leader.

Whether it's facilitating team meetings, leading a special task force, heading a charity fundraising drive, or chairing a professional association's annual conference, the more chances you have to serve in leadership roles the more likely it is that you'll develop the skills to lead—and the more likely that you'll learn the important leadership lessons that come only from the failures and successes of action.

Just any experience, however, does not support individual development by itself. Challenge is crucial to learning and career enhancement. Boring, routine jobs don't help you improve your skills and abilities. You must stretch yourself. You must seek opportunities to test yourself against new and difficult tasks. Experience *can* indeed be the best teacher—if it includes the element of personal challenge.

Whenever you select experiential activities to boost your performance, make sure you select projects and assignments that involve a stretch. If you are put in a role that doesn't stretch you, figure out how to do it differently so that you *are* stretched.

Example: Learning by Observing Others

Other people are essential sources of learning. In our research, learning from others was mentioned right behind experience as important to growth and development. We all remember the parent we looked to when wondering how to handle an unfamiliar situation, the special teacher who exhibited such joy in her vocation, the neighbor who let us help him tinker in the garage. Perhaps you had a coach who believed in you more than you believed in yourself, or a manager who treated everyone with respect and who encouraged your leadership aspirations. Role models are critical to learning anything, and they are especially important when learning how to lead.

As you think about your continuing leadership development, look around for role models, coaches, and teachers in your organization or community. Don't be shy about asking for their help or for permission to watch them at work. Ask to sit in on meetings they run or attend presentations they make. Take them out to coffee and interview them on how they handle difficult situations. Ask them to watch you in a leadership role and give you feedback.

And even though you can't observe them directly, well-known contemporary or past leaders are also excellent sources of learning. Pick up a couple of biographies and read about what these people did to become esteemed leaders.

At work, the relationship that makes the most difference in your performance is the relationship you have with your immediate manager. Managers not only serve as potential role models, but they can also provide extremely useful performance feedback. The best managers are those who challenge you, trust you, spend time with you, and teach you. Take charge of this relationship. Make the most of it. If you happen to have one of those managers who'd make a great candidate for the ten worst bosses, then observe what *not* to do. It's useful to be reminded that managers have both a positive and a negative impact on others. Adopt the positive and reject the negative.

Peers are also valuable sources of knowledge, skill, and information. Trusted peers can serve as advisers and counselors, giving you feedback on your personal style and helping you test alternative ways of dealing with problems. If you have a colleague who's strong in an area in which you're weak, ask that person to teach you what he or she knows. Ask people to share their best practices, and seek opportunities to observe them in action.

Education: Learning Through Training and Coursework

Formal training and education can definitely improve your chances of success. According to a study by the American Society for Training and Development (ASTD), "People who are trained formally in the workplace have a 30 percent higher productivity rate after one year than people who are not formally trained."

On the list of ways we learn to lead, coursework can be a high-leverage opportunity. Done right, training enables you to spend a concentrated period of time with an expert focused on one subject and only a few skills. This focused attention helps you to learn something more quickly and with the benefit of multiple chances to practice and get feedback in a safe environment.

Training also provides a safe environment for trying out new skills. Your constituents don't want you to experiment with new, untested behaviors on them, any more than you want to be on an airplane with a pilot who's never been at the controls before. Training and education provide valuable opportunities for taking some "test flights."

You should be spending at least fifty hours annually on your personal and professional development. On average, that's what Malcolm Baldrige National Quality Award-winning organizations offer their employees. In fact, Baldrige Award-winning companies in general spend about twice as much on training as the U.S. average of 1.4 percent of payroll. If you want to have this kind of success, take a cue from these companies.

For each of The Five Practices that you want to improve, commit to participating in at least one formal workshop or seminar every six months. Also take advantage of self-directed learning opportunities—an online course, for instance, that you can complete on your own time and at your own pace.

Once you've completed training, make sure you apply what you've learned. The probability that you'll apply what you've learned in training decreases with every day that passes. Once you've had that chance in training to experiment and practice, put your new learning to use immediately. Train, train, train. Then practice, practice, practice. You can't *think* that golf ball into the hole, you have to *sink* it.

Leaders Are Learners

As we mentioned earlier, in recent studies we conducted we found that there is a positive correlation between learning and leading. People who are more frequently engaged in learning activities, no matter what their learning style, perform better as leaders. This is a powerful lesson for all of us. The more we seek to learn, the better we'll become at leading—or at anything, for that matter.

We also discovered that there really is no one best way to learn. Experience, example, and education are all useful. What's clear is that the best leaders approach each new and unfamiliar experience with a willingness to learn and an appreciation of the importance of learning.

As you start to plan your development as a leader the important thing is to become a continuous learner, someone hungry for new knowledge and skills. Someone willing to experiment with new ways of doing things. To assist you in your learning, we've provided a progress review, planning tools, learning tips, suggested developmental activities, and some worksheets. More important than any of these, however, is your passion for learning. When you add your desire to the mix, becoming a better leader is not only possible, it's fun.

STEP 3

Review Your Progress and Your Feedback

Reviewing your progress, getting feedback, and making new development plans is not a one-time-only event. It is a process, one that the best leaders engage in continuously. You began that process when you reviewed your LPI Feedback Report and identified the actions you would take to move toward your ideal image of yourself as a leader. Steps 2 and 4 of this Planner are designed to help you continue the process, repeating it again and again as you improve in certain Practices and identify other areas in which you can do even better.

HOW OFTEN TO REVIEW YOUR PROGRESS AND DEVELOP NEW PLANS

Everyone's situation is different. Some people like to review their progress often; others prefer to leave several months between reviews. Here is what we suggest:

- *Informal reviews:* It's a good idea to do a quick, informal review every day. It won't take long. Just find a quiet moment to ask yourself, "How am I doing?" Then record your observations in a journal or your daily planner. Then, when it's time for a more formal review, you'll have those observations to help you assess your progress.

- *Formal reviews:* Begin by reviewing your progress and making new plans every few weeks. Later, you can increase the intervals between formal reviews if you wish. For example:

Progress Review #1—Three weeks after you receive the LPI Feedback Report

Progress Review #2—Six weeks later

Progress Review #3—Twelve weeks later

Progress Review #4 and beyond—Every quarter (twelve weeks)

The questions below will help you review your progress in carrying out your development strategies, including feedback you received while you were engaged in developmental activities, and refocus your developmental efforts.

Initial Progress Review

Begin by reviewing your progress with the commitments you made in your leadership workshop, after you first reviewed your LPI Feedback Report. Then select the leadership behaviors on which to focus during the next developmental period and make your new developmental plans. You'll need to consult your completed copy of the *Participant's Workbook* and a copy of your LPI Feedback Report, so keep them handy.

Future Progress Reviews

After six weeks, return again to these chapters. Use these questions and guidelines to review your progress and develop new plans. Return again after the next twelve weeks, or whatever interval you have selected. Each time, evaluate how well you're doing. Then identify one or two Practices and one or two behaviors related to each Practice to work on during the next developmental period.

Continue to Seek Feedback

We encourage you to seek feedback on an ongoing basis from your manager, your direct reports, your peers, and your other constituents. Use that feedback to adjust your developmental plans and develop new plans. We also suggest that you repeat the LPI at least once a year, more often if you change jobs or start to work with new constituents, to give you the detailed, structured feedback you need to continue toward your goal of becoming the best leader you can be.

1. Review Your Progress

Note: The progress review and planning pages below include check boxes and lines on which to write. You may want to re-use these pages. If you do, you have our permission to make copies for your private use.

Look at the Leadership Development Worksheet you completed in the LPI *Participant's Workbook* (pages 28–29) or in the Appendix of this Planner you completed. If this is your first progress review, also look at the Commitment Memo in the LPI *Participant's Workbook* page 35, that specifies the actions you agreed to take during the three weeks after the leadership workshop.

- To what extent did you do what you said you would do?

    ❑ Less than 25 percent

    ❑ About 50 percent

    ❑ About 75 percent

    ❑ All of it!

- If you did less than 50 percent, what stopped you? What external events, such as emergencies, got in your way? What internal obstacles, such as procrastination, kept you from doing more?

    _____

    _____

    _____

    _____

- What can you do about these kinds of obstacles?

    _____

    _____

    _____

    _____

- If you did 75 percent or more, what helped you?

  _____

  _____

  _____

- How can you capitalize on these same or other supports as you move forward?

  _____

  _____

  _____

- During this developmental period, what actions did you actually take to improve?

  _____

  _____

  _____

- In planning these actions you set some goals for yourself. To what extent did you achieve the goals that you set?

  ❑ Missed my targets completely

  ❑ Got about halfway there

  ❑ Three-quarters of the way

  ❑ Hit the center of the target

- If you missed or got only about halfway, what was off? Was it your aim or was it the target? Did you set a stretch but realistic goal, or was the goal just not achievable in the time you had? Were the actions you selected not the right ones to achieve your goals, or did you just not execute well?

  _____

  _____

  _____

- Where does all this leave you now? What do you need to continue to work on that you have already planned to do but have not done?

  _____

  _____

  _____

- What new issues came up that you need to add to your development list?

  _____

  _____

  _____

- How will you reward yourself for what you did accomplish?

  _____

  _____

  _____

2. Review Your Feedback

- As you were engaged in your developmental activities during this period, what did you learn about yourself?

  _____

  _____

  _____

- As you were engaged in your developmental activities during this period, did anyone give you feedback about how you were doing? If so, what did he or she say?

  _____

  _____

  _____

- What does the feedback you've received—from yourself and from others—tell you about the progress you're making?

  _____

  _____

  _____

  _____

- How does the feedback fit with the feedback you received from your last LPI Feedback Report?

  _____

  _____

  _____

  _____

3. Refocus Your Developmental Efforts

Now take another look at your last LPI Feedback Report, the *Participant's Workbook* from your LPI Workshop, and the last Leadership Development Worksheet you completed. Considering that information and the questions you just answered, take a fresh look at the messages people sent you and your own reflections on your leadership strengths and developmental opportunities.

- What do you now see as your strengths?

  _____

  _____

  _____

- What do you now see as your areas for improvement?

  _____

  _____

  _____

- Re-examine The Five Practices in terms of your current developmental priorities. Assign the number 1 to your top priority and 5 to your lowest priority on the list below.

  _____Model the Way

  _____Inspire a Shared Vision

  _____Challenge the Process

  _____Enable Others to Act

  _____Encourage the Heart

- Review the list of leadership behaviors on the following pages. Select a maximum of one or two Practices and one or two behaviors from each Practice on which to focus during the next developmental period. Circle those one or two Practices and one or two behaviors. Then move on to the next step, where you will develop a new plan.

Model the Way

1. I set a personal example of what I expect of others.

6. I spend time and energy making certain that the people I work with adhere to the principles and standards we have agreed on.

11. I follow through on the promises and commitments that I make.

16. I ask for feedback on how my actions affect other people's performance.

21. I build consensus around a common set of values for running our organization.

26. I am clear about my philosophy of leadership.

Inspire a Shared Vision

2. I talk about future trends that will influence how our work gets done.

7. I describe a compelling image of what our future could be like.

12. I appeal to others to share an exciting dream of the future.

17. I show others how their long-term interests can be realized by enlisting in a common vision.

22. I paint the "big picture" of what we aspire to accomplish.

27. I speak with genuine conviction about the higher meaning and purpose of our work.

Challenge the Process

3. I seek out challenging opportunities that test my own skills and abilities.

8. I challenge people to try out new and innovative ways to do their work.

13. I search outside the formal boundaries of my organization for innovative ways to improve what we do.

18. I ask "What can we learn?" when things don't go as expected.

23. I make certain that we set achievable goals, make concrete plans, and establish measurable milestones for the projects and programs that we work on.

28. I experiment and take risks, even when there is a chance of failure.

Enable Others to Act

4. I develop cooperative relationships among the people I work with.

9. I actively listen to diverse points of view.

14. I treat others with dignity and respect.

19. I support the decisions that people make on their own.

24. I give people a great deal of freedom and choice in deciding how to do their work.

29. I ensure that people grow in their jobs by learning new skills and developing themselves.

Encourage the Heart

5. I praise people for a job well done.

10. I make it a point to let people know about my confidence in their abilities.

15. I make sure that people are creatively rewarded for their contributions to the success of our projects.

20. I publicly recognize people who exemplify commitment to shared values.

25. I find ways to celebrate accomplishments.

30. I give the members of the team lots of appreciation and support for their contributions.

People WHO BECOME leaders DON'T *always* **seek** THE challenges THEY Face. CHALLENGES *also* SEEK leaders.

STEP 4

Make New Plans

Once you've selected the leadership behaviors on which to focus during the upcoming development period, you will make your new development plans. As you did when you developed your first plan in the leadership workshop, begin with a description of your ideal self as a leader. Then think about what stands in your way and how you are leveraging your strengths. Finally, complete a new Leadership Development Worksheet and make your new commitments public.

1. Review Your Description of "My Ideal Self As a Leader"

Review the last description you wrote of your ideal self as a leader. For instance, as one of your developmental areas let's say you selected the behavior, "I describe a compelling image of what our future could be like." When you imagined yourself two years from now doing just that, you might have written: "Whenever I talk about our company's direction, people will comment on how positive and enthusiastic I am about our future; I will become more personally peaceful by not letting the little things I can't control detract me from the work; I will be realistic about facts but confident about possibilities, etc."

Now think about how your expectations for yourself have changed. Given the Practices and behaviors on which you now want to focus your developmental efforts, imagine that you're executing them significantly more effectively than you are currently. Write a positive statement that describes the situation and the way you will be behaving two years from now that reflects those changed expectations.

_____

_____

_____

_____

_____

_____

_____

_____

_____

_____

2. Overcome Barriers And Leverage Strengths

Re-evaluate obstacles that are preventing you from achieving your ideal image and identify actions you could take to build on your strengths.

- What gets in your way right now of achieving your ideal image? Check any of the following that might be creating barriers for you:

  _____ Lack of skills

  _____ Lack of training and development opportunities

  _____ Absence of a supportive manager or climate

  _____ Limited access to good role models

_____ Few opportunities to take on challenging assignments

_____ Fear of losing control of your team

_____ Fear of being seen as weak

_____ Fear that if you rock the boat it will be seen as a threat to the hierarchy

Other barriers:

_____

_____

_____

_____

_____

_____

• What actions could you take to overcome these barriers?

_____

_____

_____

_____

_____

• How can you leverage and build on your strengths to overcome the barriers and make yourself an even better leader?

_____

_____

_____

_____

_____

_____

3. Choose Developmental Actions

Considering what you have identified as your priorities and the expectations you have for yourself, what actions can help you learn to be a better leader?

- What experiences do you need in order to achieve your ideal image?

  _____

  _____

  _____

  _____

  _____

- Who can serve as an example to help you achieve your ideal image?

  _____

  _____

  _____

  _____

  _____

- What education and training do you need to achieve your ideal image?

  _____

  _____

  _____

  _____

  _____

4. Make a Plan

Now, fill out the Leadership Development Worksheet on the next page, in order to make your plan for the next developmental period. A sample worksheet is provided to assist you. (Additional worksheets are provided in Part II.)

To stimulate your thinking about the kinds of actions you can take, consult the Ways to Improve Your Leadership Practices in Part II of this Planner. Select the Practice on which you want to work, and then turn to those pages in Resource B.

LEADERSHIP DEVELOPMENT WORKSHEET
Sample

Today's Date: May 1, 2003

Leadership Development Period from May 1 **to** May 22, 2003

Leadership Practice Focus: _Inspire a Shared Vision_

Leadership Behavior Focus: 7. Describes a compelling image of the future

Measurements of Progress:
Turn your ideal image into measurable goals

I will know that I reached my improvement goal for the next three weeks when:

- I have written a 5 to 7 minute presentation of my vision
- My colleague, Terry, gives me feedback that he finds my statement "compelling"
- My direct reports give me feedback that my vision statement is at least a 3 on a scale of 1 (not at all compelling) to 5 (i'll sign up!)

Primary Development Strategy:

Circle one primary strategy from among these three basic approaches to learning and development:

Action Steps:

Using your primary strategy, what actions do you need to take to achieve your ideal image—your measurable goals?

- Experience
- Example
- Education

- Write a 5 to 7 minute vision statement

- Make sure to include metaphors, examples, and other relevant imagery in my vision statement
- Sit down with Terry, who does this better than anyone I know, and share what I have written. Get his feedback. Make changes accordingly and review with him again
- Present the vision statement to my team and ask for their honest feedback
- Revise again

Secondary Developmental Strategy:

- Experience
- Example
- Education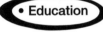

Action Steps:

- Listen to Martin Luther King, Jr.'s "I have a dream" speech and take notes on what he does to enlist others—his methods and content.
- Read chapter 6 in Jim Kouzes and Barry Posner's book, The Leadership Challenge, on "Enlist Others."

LEADERSHIP DEVELOPMENT WORKSHEET

Today's Date: _____

Leadership Development Period from _____ **to** _____

Leadership Practice Focus: _____

Leadership Behavior Focus: _____

Measurements of Progress:
Turn your ideal image into
measurable goals

_____

_____

_____

_____

_____

_____

_____

_____

_____

Primary Development
Strategy:
Circle one primary strategy
from among these three
basic approaches to
learning and development:

Action Steps:

Using your primary strategy, what actions
do you need to take to achieve your ideal
image—your measurable goals?

• Experience

_____

_____

_____

• Example

_____

• Education

_____

_____

_____

_____

_____

_____

_____

_____

_____

_____

_____

Secondary Developmental Strategy:

Circle a secondary strategy

- Experience

- Example

- Education

Action Steps:

_____

_____

_____

_____

_____

_____

_____

_____

_____

_____

5. *Make Your Commitments Public*

Your last step is to make your new commitments public. Telling at least one other person what you intend to do is a way to help ensure that you'll follow through. Tell your manager, your coach, or close colleague what actions you intend to take, and by when you will take them. Make an agreement with that person to get together at a certain time to review your progress.

STEP 5

First, Lead Yourself

There's a scene in the film adaptation of Muriel Spark's classic, *The Prime of Miss Jean Brodie,* during which Headmistress McKay calls Miss Brodie to her office to chastise Miss Brodie for her somewhat unorthodox teaching methods. Headmistress McKay comments on the precocity of Miss Brodie's students. Miss Brodie accepts this as a compliment, not a criticism, and says:

> "To me education is a leading out. The word education comes from the root 'ex,' meaning 'out,' and 'duco,' 'I lead.' To me education is simply a leading out of what is already there."

To this Headmistress McKay responds rather haughtily, saying, "I had hoped there might also be a certain amount of putting in."

Miss Brodie laughs at this notion and replies, "That would not be education, but intrusion."

We agree. The process of development should never be intrusive. It should never be about filling someone full of facts or skills. Education should always be liberating. It should always be about releasing what is already inside.

The quest for leadership is first an inner quest to discover who you are. Through self-development comes the confidence needed to lead. Self-confidence is really awareness of and faith in your own powers. These powers become clear and strong only as you work to identify and develop them.

Learning to lead is about discovering what *you* care about and value. About what inspires *you*. About what challenges *you*. About what gives *you* power and competence. About what encourages *you*. When you discover these things about yourself, you'll know what it takes to lead those qualities out of others.

Sure, we've said that every leader has to learn the fundamentals and the discipline, and to a certain extent there's some period during which you're trying out a lot of new things. It's a necessary stage in your development as a leader. The point is that you have to take what's been acquired and reshape it into your own expression of yourself.

Sometimes liberation is as uncomfortable as intrusion, but in the end when you discover things for yourself you know that what's inside is what you found there and what belongs there. It's not something put inside you by someone else; it's what you discover for yourself.

We wish you continuing joy and success on your leadership learning adventures.

PART II

Selecting Leadership Development Resources

RESOURCE A

Ten Tips for Becoming a Better Leader

We asked a number of leaders and leadership coaches to share with us their best learning practices for becoming a better leader. We combined their observations with our own and others' research and synthesized these lessons into the following top ten tips. Use them as you review your progress and continue your leadership development efforts.

TIP #1. BE SELF-AWARE

There's solid evidence that the best leaders are highly attuned to what's going on inside of them as they are leading. They're very self-aware. They're also quite aware of the impact they're having on others. In fact, self-awareness may be the most crucial learning skill of all.

Think about it this way. Let's say you begin to hear an odd sound every time you start your car. You ignore it, and pretty soon you don't even notice it any more. You just keep on driving. Then one day your car won't start at all. The mechanic tells you that it would have been a simple, inexpensive problem to fix if you had paid attention when it first started, but because you ignored it for so long, it's going to cost a bundle.

The same is true in leading. Self-awareness helps you receive clues about what's going on inside you and in your environment.

Your emotions are messages. They're trying to teach you something. Don't be afraid of them, and don't become self-conscious about them. Just listen and learn. Take time to reflect on your experiences. Keep a journal of some kind, or record your thoughts and feelings on tape. As you go through your developmental experiences, look within yourself and pay attention to how you're feeling.

TIP #2. MANAGE YOUR EMOTIONS

While the best leaders are self-aware, they are careful not to let their feelings manage them. Instead, they manage their feelings.

Self-control is important. Let's say you become aware that you get angry when people are unprepared for a meeting. One way to respond would be to yell at them and put them down in front of the group. But would that be the best way to handle the situation for the sake of your credibility and your relationship with your constituents? No, it would not.

The same is true in learning. There will be times when you become frustrated and when you become upset at the feedback that you receive. You could go out and break something or yell at someone, but that won't help your learning or your relationships. So manage your emotions. Be aware of them, but don't let them rule your behavior. And if you sense that you need help managing those emotions, seek it.

TIP #3. SEEK FEEDBACK

One of the reasons the best leaders are highly self-aware is that they ask for feedback from others. In fact, the best leaders ask for feedback not only about what they're doing well, but about what they're not doing well. They want to know the negative as well as the positive.

Now you can understand why being able to manage your emotions is so important. Who in his right mind is going to give you negative feedback if he knows you're going to get angry? But if people know you genuinely want the feedback, that you'll thank them for it, and that you'll do something with the feedback they give you, then you'll benefit, and so will they.

When people are learning, others tend to be very forgiving. So tell your constituents what you're trying to do and that you want their honest feedback. Afterward, ask, "How'd I do?" Have a conversation. Then say thanks.

TIP #4. TAKE THE INITIATIVE

Our research is very clear on this point: The best leaders are proactive. They don't wait for someone else to tell them what to do. They take the initiative to find and solve problems and to meet and create challenges. The same is true in learning.

The best leaders don't wait to be told by a manager or by someone in human resources that they need to change their behavior. Instead, they take charge of their own learning. Because they're self-aware and they seek feedback, they know their strengths and weaknesses, and they know what needs to be done. They seek the developmental opportunities they need. If the resources aren't available from the organization, they find a way to get the experience, example, or education some other way.

It's your learning. It's your career. It's your life. Take charge of it.

TIP #5. ENGAGE A COACH

The top athletes, the top musicians, and the top performing artists all have coaches. Leadership is a performing art, too, and the best leaders also have coaches. The coach might be someone from inside or outside of the organization. She might be a peer, a manager, a trainer, or someone with specific expertise in what you are trying to learn. Coaches can play a number of roles. The most obvious is to watch you perform, give you feedback, and offer suggestions for improvement. But effective coaches can also be a very valuable source of social support, which is essential to resilience and persistence. Support is especially important when people are being asked to change their behavior. When you return to work after training, your initial enthusiasm can be quickly crushed if there is no one around to offer words of encouragement. Every leader needs someone to lean on from time to time. Your coach should be able to offer you not only advice but also attention and caring. Also, the best coaches are good listeners. In fact, they watch and listen about twice as much as they teach and tell.

We've found in our research on coaching that the factor most related to coaching effectiveness is the quality of the relationship between performer and coach. And of all the items used to measure coaching behavior, the one most linked to success is: "This person embodies character qualities and values that I admire." (There's that credibility factor again.)

TIP #6. SET GOALS AND MAKE A PLAN

Exemplary leaders make sure that the work they do to develop themselves is not pointless ambling but purposeful action. Too often people participate in training and development without any clear goals in mind. They never ask themselves: "Why am I here?" "What do I want to get out of this learning experience?" People who attend training programs with a clear sense of what they want to accomplish are much more likely to apply what they learn than those who do not have clear goals. Leadership development has a purpose, and that purpose should be clear to everyone.

Set high expectations for yourself and for your constituents. Adults in the workplace and children in school tend to perform to the level of expectations. The leaders who are the most successful at bringing out the best in others set achievable stretch goals—that is, they set goals that are high, but not so far out of reach that people give up even before they start because they think, "I can never do that." Leaders who succeed in getting high performance also display confidence in other people's abilities to perform. The research is crystal clear: Leaders who say, "I know you can do it," get better results. And leaders who bring out the best in others also believe in their own abilities to coach and train. You have to have confidence in yourself as well as confidence in others to be a good coach. These same principles apply to learning.

It's important to make your goals public. You are more likely to work harder to improve if you tell other people what you're trying to accomplish than if you keep it to yourself. There is always less commitment when goals are kept private.

Once you've set your goals, make a plan. Figure out the steps from where you are to where you want to be. There may be several options available, just as there are several routes you could take to travel across the country—you just need to pick the one that best suits your needs.

In setting your goals and making your plans, focus on a few things at a time. You may have a strong desire to improve in three of The Five Practices and in ten of the thirty behaviors. That's terrific, but don't attempt to do everything at once. The fact is that most improvements are incremental. Take it one step at a time. There are no such things as "conversions" to great leadership.

TIP #7. PRACTICE, PRACTICE, PRACTICE

People who practice more often are more likely to become experts at what they do. To be the best you can be, you must not only apply what you learn on the playing field, but you must also hone your skills on the practice field. We know this is true in the performing arts and in sports, but somehow we do not always apply the same idea to leadership. Professional leaders take practice seriously. The practice may be role playing a negotiation, rehearsing a speech, or a one-on-one dialogue with a coach. Whatever it is, practice is essential to learning.

Practice fields also offer the opportunity to try out unfamiliar methods, behaviors, and tools in a safer environment than on-the-job situations. You are more likely to take risks when you feel safe than when you feel highly vulnerable. Since the stakes are higher on the job than on the practice field, give yourself the chance to run some plays in practice before rushing into the game.

You can also treat every experience as a learning experience, even when it's for real. Whether you consider the experience a raving success or a miserable failure, step back and ask yourself and those involved, "What went well? What went poorly?" "What did I do well? What did I do poorly?" "What could we improve?" The best leaders are the best learners, and learning can occur any time, anywhere. Take advantage of that fact.

TIP #8. MEASURE PROGRESS

People need to know whether they're making progress or marking time. Goals help to serve that function, but goals alone are not enough. It's not enough to know that you want to make it to the summit. You also need to know whether you're still climbing, or whether you're sliding downhill.

Measuring progress is crucial to improvement, no matter what the activity. Whether it's strengthening endurance, shedding pounds, increasing sales, or becoming a better leader, knowing how well you've done in terms of the goals you've set is crucial to motivation and achievement. Setting goals without feedback is actually no better in improving performance than setting no goals at all. It's the two together that propel performance forward.

Exemplary leaders and exemplary learners create a system that enables them to monitor and measure progress on a regular basis. The best measurement systems are ones that are visible and instant—like the speedometer on your dashboard or the watch on your wrist. The best measurement systems are also ones that you can check yourself, without having to wait for someone else to tell you. For instance, you can count how many thank-you notes you send out by keeping a log.

A self-monitoring system can include asking for feedback. Others may need to give you the information about how you're doing, but you're in charge of the asking. Another way to monitor your progress is to repeat the administration of the *Leadership Practices Inventory* once or twice a year.

TIP #9. REWARD YOURSELF

If new behavior is not rewarded, that behavior will be quickly forgotten. Even worse, when you say you want new behavior but actually reward the *old* behavior, people quickly conclude that you are not serious about the new behavior. For example, let's say you want to create a greater sense of teamwork among your salesforce, but instead of setting up a new incentive system that rewards teamwork, you continue to reward people solely on the basis of who sells the most. It's likely that your salespeople will continue the behavior that gets rewarded.

Connect your performance to rewards. It's nice when others recognize you for your efforts, but that doesn't always happen. So along with the goals that you set and the measurement system that you put in place, make sure to create some ways to reward yourself for achieving your goals. Take yourself out to lunch—and ask a good friend to go with you. Mark the achievement in red pen in your calendar, knowing that every time you look at it you'll get a big smile on your face for accomplishing something. Brag about it to a colleague. Use one of your regular meetings to announce your progress to your team. They *will* applaud. It's okay to toot your own horn every now and then. By the way, it's also okay to ask others for positive feedback: "Tell me something I did well today." You need that, too.

TIP #10. BE HONEST WITH YOURSELF AND HUMBLE WITH OTHERS

We know from our research that credibility is the foundation of leadership, and honesty is at the top of the list of what constituents look for in a leader. What does honesty have to do with learning to lead?

Everything. You can't become better at something unless you're able to recognize and accept your strengths and your weaknesses. In our research we have yet to encounter a leader who scores a perfect 10 on every behavior. We all can improve, and the first step is understanding what most needs improving. We don't mean you're supposed to beat yourself up over faults and mistakes; just be intellectually and emotionally honest.

Being honest means that you're willing to admit mistakes, own up to your faults, and be open to suggestions for improvement. It also means that you're accepting of the same in others. We're by no means saying that it's okay for you and others to repeat the *same* mistake over and over again. The point is simply that neither you nor anyone can improve without being willing to admit to and to accept error as part of the improvement process.

Honesty with yourself and others also produces a level of humility that earns you credibility. People don't respect know-it-alls, especially when they know that the know-it-all *doesn't* know it all. People like people who show they are human. Admitting mistakes and being open to accepting new ideas and new learning communicates that you are willing to grow. It does something else as well. It promotes a culture of honesty and openness. That's healthy for you and for others.

Hubris is the killer disease in leadership. It's fun to be a leader, gratifying to have influence, and exhilarating to have scores of people cheering your every word. In many all-too-subtle ways, it's easy to be seduced by power and importance. All evil leaders have been infected with the disease of hubris, becoming bloated with an exaggerated sense of self and pursuing their own sinister ends. How then to avoid it?

Humility is the only way to resolve the conflicts and contradictions of leadership. You can avoid excessive pride only if you recognize that you're human and need the help of others, and that's an important reason for leaders being great learners.

Somewhere,

s o m e t i m e ,

THE *leader* **within**

EACH OF US

MAY **get**

THE CALL

to STEP forward.

RESOURCE B

Ways to Improve Your Leadership Practices

With the help of the LPI, you have been given the gift of feedback about your leadership practices, and with the help of this leadership development experience, you have begun the process of improving in those practices you identified as your weaker areas. In the first two chapters of this Planner, you have examined the ways in which people learn to lead and the top ten best learning practices of exemplary leaders.

Learning to lead is a lifelong pursuit. The more we learn, the more we realize how little we know. Sustaining your self-development on an ongoing basis requires continuing to seek opportunities to learn. In this chapter, we've suggested developmental activities for each of The Five Practices—pick and choose what's right for you and add your own. You can return to this list again and again, every time you want ideas about how to keep learning to be a better leader.

ACTIVITIES FOR IMPROVING IN ALL FIVE PRACTICES

The self-development activities in the list below will help you improve in any of The Five Practices.

Learning from Experience

- Seek opportunities to engage in leadership behaviors. Make speeches. Be a mentor. Coach a team. Volunteer to manage challenging projects or help community groups find innovative ways to raise funds.

Learning from Examples

- Keep a journal. Record your observations about what exemplary leaders do to Model the Way, Inspire a Shared Vision, Challenge the Process, Enable Others to Act, and Encourage the Heart. Review your journal regularly, especially when you are developing your own action plans.

- Read biographies and watch videos and films of exemplary leaders. Listen to exemplary leaders' speeches. Notice what leaders do that makes them successful.

- Interview leaders you admire and respect. Ask for permission to observe them in their day-to-day activities. Try to identify what they do to lead successfully. Ask for their advice on becoming a successful leader.

Learning from Education

- Continue to take classes and self-learning programs to expand your knowledge and skills in specific areas.

- Learn to use technology that will help you automate processes, organize your activities, and stay focused on your goals.

- Work with coaches to improve in specific areas.

Improving in Model the Way

Leaders establish values about how constituents, colleagues, and customers ought to be treated. They create standards of excellence and set an example for others to follow. If you have identified Model the Way as one of the practices in which you need to improve, here are some actions you can take.

Learning from Experience

- Write a statement that clarifies your personal credo—the values or principles that you believe should guide your part of the organization. Communicate your credo orally and in writing to your key constituents. Post it prominently for everyone to see. Start each values statement with the phrase, "I value . . ." and then fill in the rest. For example: "I value teamwork—we're all in this together" "I value uncompromising customer service" "I value cutting-edge innovation" "I value dedication to family" or "I value fun." Limit your list to no more than seven items—it's hard to keep track of more than seven, and it's important to set priorities. Also, express the items in *your own words*. You will have to be the one to speak them and put them into practice.

- Think about the times you've made sacrifices or felt at a crossroads in your life. What values guided your choices?

- Answer this question: "What would make you weep?" What does your answer say about what you care deeply about?

- Ask others on your team to write their credos and share them at a meeting. Ask team members to come to consensus about the values they're prepared to live out in their work. Compare your values to the team's, and to the organization's. If there's any incompatibility, resolve it.

  It might be possible for you to live out one or more of your values without the rest of the team sharing them. For example, let's say you value fun at work, but you find that most of the other team members do not share this value. Ask yourself, "Is this something that must be a shared value for me to be committed to the organization?" "Can I live without it?" "Can I find ways to live out this value without it being shared?"

  On the other hand, you might feel that you cannot commit to the organization without others sharing certain values. For example, if teamwork is an important value to you and is not shared, you will have to engage in a dialogue with other team members. The first step is to let others know: "This is important to me and I can't commit fully in an environment that doesn't stress teamwork." If you can't find common ground, then you may want to consider whether this is the right place for you.

- Keep a log to track how you spend your time. Check to see whether your daily activities are consistent with your team's values and with your own. Figure out what you need to do to resolve any inconsistencies.

- Set a personal example for others by behaving in ways that demonstrate and reinforce your values and those of your organization. If collaboration is a value in your organization, for example, make sure that you act as a team player. You might pitch in to do some selling if that is required. If your team is working late on a project, then you should also be working late—and you might volunteer to go out and get the pizza for dinner. You might help out on the loading dock. You might include teamwork in performance reviews.

- Learn to say "yes" and "no." For instance, if top quality is your priority, say "no" to every flaw you notice. If you're invited to give a talk on quality, say "yes." Conviction and consistency in saying "yes" and "no" tell people how serious you really are.

- Develop a list of questions you can ask to find out whether your team members are living out the team's values. Ask these questions at staff meetings. For example, ask people what they've done in the last week to make sure their work is top quality.

- Include values in performance appraisals. Make sure that you and others are evaluated according to how well you live out your values.

- Be expressive—even emotional—about your beliefs. If you're proud of your staff for living up to high performance standards, let them know. Brag about them to others.

- Keep your daily planner at hand so you can write down promises as you make them. Review your promises daily and fulfill them on schedule. Be sure to let others know that you've done what you said you'd do.

- Do something dramatic to demonstrate your commitment to a team value. For instance, if creativity is a value, take everyone to a local toy store, buy some children's games, and spend a couple of hours playing them. Then discuss what people learned about creativity that could be applied to their own work or to the organization as a whole.

- When you make a mistake or things don't go as planned, how do you behave? What do you say? Do your deeds match your words? How do you make sure that you use critical incidents as learning experiences?

- Focus on the little things—not just the big ones—so that people know you value the quality of their work lives. Fixing a leaky roof is just as important as constructing a beautiful new building. What "leaky roofs" are there around your organization, and what can you do to fix them? For example, maybe the interior of your office needs a fresh coat of paint. Paint it. Maybe the pictures on the wall are old and faded. Put up new ones. Maybe nobody has ever sat down and talked with individual team members about what they are working on in the organization. Spend one hour with each person on this question. These little things matter, and they add up.

- Imagine that two years from now you'll be named an "exemplary leader" in your profession. What will the person presenting this award say about you? Write that introduction.

- Imagine that two years from now you and your work group will be named "Team of the Year." What will the person introducing this award say about the values that your team exemplified? Write this introduction.

- What else could you do to clarify your own and others' values?

  _____
  _____
  _____
  _____

- What else could you do to communicate and build consensus around values?

  _____
  _____
  _____
  _____

- In what other ways could you personally set an example of your team's values?

  _____
  _____
  _____
  _____

- What else could you do to learn from experience in Model the Way?

_____

_____

_____

Learning from Examples

- Watch the film *Gandhi* with some colleagues. Afterward, discuss how Gandhi set an example for his constituents.

- Choose several other well-known leaders whom you consider to be role models. Learn what they did (or what they do) to be successful leaders by reading their biographies or watching films about them.

- Identify the person in your own life—not a famous leader, but someone you know—whom you consider to be your number one leadership role model. What did or does this person stand for? How do you know this? How does this person act on what she or he stands for? Now apply this same exercise to yourself: How do people know what you stand for?

- Ask several trusted colleagues to choose the two or three people in your organization they consider to be the most credible. Interview these people. Spend time with them. Observe what they do in their leadership roles.

- Observe others to see whether their words and deeds are consistent. Look for actions that indicate they are living out their values. Also look for contradictions. Notice what happens when people's words and deeds are consistent, and when they are inconsistent.

- Visit a retail store that is widely acknowledged for its extraordinary customer service. Watch and listen to what the store employees do and say. Shop there and see how you're treated. Interview some of the employees about what people do to maintain the store's stellar reputation.

- Think of two or three people you have known personally whom you respect and trust—coaches, teachers, bosses, friends. In your journal, describe your reasons for feeling that way about each person.

- Spend some time with someone you personally look to as a role model. Observe what that person does. Ask him or her for advice on how to make behavior consistent with values.

- What else could you do to learn from example in Model the Way?

_____

_____

_____

Learning from Education

- Take a class or a self-directed learning program in clarifying personal values.

- Take a time management course. Then analyze how consistent your activities are with your values.

- Take a story-telling class. Tell stories about people living out their values every time you get the opportunity.

- Take a course in goal setting and action planning. Apply what you learn to setting your own goals and developing your own action plans. Help your team do the same.

- What other classes, self-directed learning programs, or educational activities can you use to help you improve in Model the Way?

_____

_____

_____

Improving in Inspire a Shared Vision

Leaders are futurists. They imagine what they and their organization can become, and then they enlist others in their shared dreams. Here are some actions you can take to improve in Inspire a Shared Vision.

Learning from Experience

- Become a futurist. Join the World Futures Society. Read *American Demographics* or other magazines about future trends. Use the Internet to find a "futures" conference that you can attend. Make a list of what reputable people are predicting will happen in the next ten years. Look for patterns in these trends and figure out how your organization will be affected.

- Ask yourself, "Am I in the job to do something or am I in it for something to do?" If your answer is "To do something"—which we assume it will be—write down what you want to accomplish in your current job and why. Make sure you can answer this question: "Five years from now, if someone asks what I have accomplished in this job, what will I say?"

- Put your feet up, close your eyes, and visualize yourself five years in the future. What will you be doing? What will those you work with be doing? What will your family be doing? What differences will there be in the ways that people work and live? Get as clear a picture as possible. Then repeat the process, extending the timeline to ten years.

- Imagine that it is ten years from now. Write a 1,000-word article that explains how you have made a difference during the last decade—how you've contributed to your job, your organization, your family, your community.

- Interview some of your key constituents about their hopes, dreams, goals, and aspirations for the future. How do these relate to your own? How can you incorporate their aspirations into yours?

- Meet with your constituents and ask them to share their hopes and dreams with one another. Ask them to listen carefully and identify common goals. Make those common goals visible by writing them on a flip-chart page and posting the page where everyone can see it.

- Turn what you imagine about the future into a five- to ten-minute "vision speech" for your organization. Keep the written speech in your daily planner. Review it daily, revising and refining it as you feel moved to do so.

- Read your vision speech to someone who will give you constructive feedback. Ask, "Is this speech imaginative or conservative?" "Is it unique or ordinary?" "Does it evoke visual images?" "Is it oriented toward the future or toward the present?" "Does it offer a view that can be shared by others?"

- Consciously use more stories, examples, and imagery when you describe the future in your conversations. People can visualize something much better when you use language in this way, so try doing it as often as you can.

- Deliver your vision speech at every opportunity: At team meetings, at company meetings, at club meetings, at home. Publish it and disseminate it widely. Ask people for feedback. Ask them if they could see themselves as part of this future.

- Regularly set aside time to talk about the future with your staff. Make your vision of the future an ongoing part of staff meetings, working lunches, conversations by the coffee machine, and so on.

- Hang out where your constituents hang out. Visit the research lab, the distribution center, the retail stores. Go to the neighborhoods, the restaurants, the coffee shops, and your constituents' clubs. Travel to the countries where you have operations and customers. Absorb the culture and the atmosphere. Walk in your constituents' shoes, and try to imagine the future they want for themselves and their families.

- Whenever possible, volunteer to stand up in front of a group and speak, even if it's just to introduce someone or make an announcement. The more you practice public speaking, the more comfortable you will become, and the better you will be at Inspire a Shared Vision.

- What else could you do to clarify the kind of future you'd like people to create together?

_____

_____

_____

_____

_____

_____

- What else could you do to forecast what the future will be like or to scan for future trends?

_____

_____

_____

_____

_____

_____

- What else could you do to learn more about your constituents' needs and aspirations?

_____

_____

_____

_____

_____

_____

- What else could you do to become more expressive in your communications?

_____

_____

_____

_____

_____

_____

- What else could you do to improve in Inspire a Shared Vision?

_____

_____

_____

_____

_____

_____

Learning from Examples

- Read biographies of people who are considered to be visionary. A few examples are Walt Disney, Katharine Graham, Thomas Jefferson, Susan B. Anthony, Herb Kelleher, Anita Roddick—there are many, many more.

- Listen to speeches by exemplary leaders who've inspired a shared vision. One example is Martin Luther King, Jr.'s, "I Have a Dream" speech. Learn everything you can from the masters.

- Attend a lecture given by an inspirational speaker. Notice what the speaker does to express himself or herself with conviction and enthusiasm. If you attend a presentation where the speaker fails to inspire or connect with the audience, make notes on what *not* to do.

- Interview a speech writer. Ask him or her to share methods for constructing an inspirational speech.

- Go to a concert or an opera. Observe how the conductor uses his or her body and energy to bring forth the best in others.

- What else could you do to learn from examples in Inspire a Shared Vision?

_____

_____

_____

_____

_____

_____

_____

_____

Learning from Education

- Read books about inspiring shared visions.

- Join Toastmasters and/or take a course in giving effective presentations.

- Take a public speaking course.

- Take a course in interpersonal communication skills.

- Take singing and/or acting lessons.

- What other classes or educational opportunities could help you improve in Inspire a Shared Vision?

_____

_____

_____

_____

_____

_____

_____

_____

_____

_____

_____

_____

Improving in Challenge the Process

Leaders search for opportunities to change the status quo and seek innovative ways to improve their organizations. They experiment and take risks, accepting the inevitable disappointments as learning opportunities. To avoid being overwhelmed by complex change—and avoid overwhelming others—leaders take change one step at a time. Following are some suggestions on how to improve in Challenge the Process.

Learning from Experience

- Volunteer for a tough assignment in your workplace or your community. Be proactive in looking for chances to stretch yourself and learn something new.

- Treat every day as if it were your first day at work, bringing brand-new challenges. Ask yourself, "What can I do today so that I will do my job better and smarter than I did yesterday?"

- Make a list of every task you perform. About each task, ask yourself, "Why am I doing this?" "Why am I doing it this way?" "Can this task be eliminated or done significantly better?"

- Begin your next staff meeting with the following question: "What action did you take last week to make your performance even better this week?" Persist in asking this question for at least three meetings in a row so that everyone knows you're serious about continual improvement. Be prepared to answer this same question for yourself at each meeting.

- Devote at least 25 percent of staff meeting time to seeking ways to improve processes and develop new products or services.

- About every policy and procedure in your organization or unit, ask: "Why are we doing it this way?" If the answer is, "Because we've always done it this way," respond with "How is it contributing to making us the best we can be?" If you don't get a satisfactory answer, eliminate or significantly improve the process or procedure so that it does contribute.

- Ask employees what annoys them about the organization or unit. Commit to changing three of the most frequently mentioned items that are hindering success.

- Go shopping for ideas. Visit local businesses—anything from restaurants to machine shops. Bring back at least one thing that each business does very well and that your organization could copy. Then adapt this idea to your organization and implement the change.

- Identify a process in your organization that's broken—your compensation system, your sales strategy, your order-fulfillment process. Whatever it is, take action to fix it.

- Set up a pilot project for an innovative way of doing something: Try out a new merchandising approach, streamline the billing system, change the way work shifts are scheduled. Evaluate the pilot, learn from it, and try it again.

- When someone in your group makes a mistake, find a way to turn the inevitable mistakes of innovation into a learning experience. For example, let's say that someone has an innovative idea about how to market a new service using the Web. Your team goes all out to try the idea, but after six months it has produced few leads and no sales. You certainly don't want to punish the person with the idea, and you shouldn't ignore the failure either. Instead, bring the entire project to a "seminar" with your team and have them analyze it, much as they would a business school case: "Why didn't this idea work out as planned?" "What factors might explain it?" "What can we learn from this so that we can do better the next time?"

- When you make a mistake yourself, admit it and then tell people what you learned from the failure. It sets an example for others that it's okay to try something new, fail, and then learn from it.

- Reward risk takers. Praise them. Give them prizes. Give them the opportunity to talk about their experiences and share the lessons they've learned. It's money in the bank.

- Set goals for the team and for each member that are achievable, given the circumstances. An unachievable goal is something that is outside the current capacity of the team. For instance, "We'll quadruple sales this quarter" might not be achievable because of time, budget, and people restraints. Doubling sales, on the other hand, may very well be achievable. Tell people what the key milestones are so that they can easily see their progress.

- After the completion of significant milestones and projects, conduct a "post-mortem"—a meeting in which people talk about what went well, what didn't go so well, what they learned, and what they'd do differently the next time.

- Stand up for your beliefs, even if you're a minority of one.

- What else can you do to challenge the status quo?

_____

_____

_____

_____

_____

_____

_____

- What else can you do to experiment with new ways of doing things?

  _____

  _____

  _____

  _____

- In addition to rewards, what else can you do to support people as they seek challenging opportunities and experiment with new ways of doing things?

  _____

  _____

  _____

  _____

- What else could you do to set clear goals, make plans, and establish milestones for the projects you lead?

  _____

  _____

  _____

  _____

Learning from Examples

- Identify some successful people in your organization who excel at Challenge the Process. Ask them what they think are the ingredients for innovation and experimentation, what they do when they encounter obstacles, and how they "get away with" challenging the status quo. Do the same with some people in other organizations.

- Follow some challengers as they go about their daily activities. Make notes about what they do to Challenge the Process.

- Read about revolutionaries in business, science, politics, religion, or any other endeavor. In your journal, record what you learned from the accounts of their lives, especially what they did when they ran up against an obstacle.

- What else could you do to learn from example in Challenge the Process?

_____

_____

_____

_____

_____

_____

Learning from Education

- Take a course in creative problem solving.

- Take a course in new product development.

- Take a course in entrepreneurship.

- Spend time in an Outward Bound or similar wilderness-adventure program.

- Take a class in a subject you know nothing about or take lessons to learn something you do not know how to do—speak Italian, play tennis, or other activities. Keep a journal in which you record your observations about how it feels to go through the learning process.

- Find a coach to help you become even better at something you already do well—make a stronger presentation, lower your golf handicap, cook a gourmet meal. Record what you learned from the experience in your journal.

- What else could you do to challenge yourself and experience new things?

  _____

  _____

  _____

  _____

  _____

  _____

Improving in Enable Others to Act

Leaders foster collaboration and actively involve others, striving to create an atmosphere of trust and human dignity. They strengthen others, sharing their power and seeking ways to make others feel capable and powerful. Here are suggestions for developing your abilities in this Practice.

Learning from Experience

- Find ways to increase interactions among people who need to work more effectively together. Teamwork and trust can only be built when people interact informally as well as formally. Establish common meeting areas that encourage people to interact. Put the coffee pot and popcorn maker in a location between groups that should talk with one other. Ask people from other parts of the organization to attend your regular staff meetings. Schedule a lunch for two groups that don't spend much time face-to-face.

- Treat every job as a project involving people from a variety of functions instead of a linear series of tasks. Ask yourself which people should be involved, and involve them all from the beginning.

- Commit to replacing the word "I" with "we." As a leader you can't do the job alone; extraordinary things are accomplished as a result of group efforts, not individual efforts. "We" is an inclusive word that signals a commitment to teamwork and sharing. Use it liberally.

- Replace the word "subordinate" with "associate" or "team member."

- Volunteer to be the chairperson of a professional, civic, or industry association. Working with volunteers will teach you collaborative skills and give you opportunities to use them.

- Assign important tasks to others. For example, if a presentation to a key customer is coming up, ask a promising young staff member to prepare the presentation and deliver it, with your assistance as coach.

- Assign non-routine work to people who often do routine work. Routine work breeds a sense of being powerless, whereas non-routine work fosters a sense of doing something important.

- Regularly ask co-workers for their opinions and viewpoints. Share problems with them.

- Make sure that everyone in your organization or unit receives at least forty hours of job-related training each year.

- Hang out at the coffee machine first thing in the morning. Engage in conversations about how things are going in your associates' lives outside of work. This is not about prying into people's private lives, but about showing genuine interest in people who have lives other than work. The more you know about their families, their hobbies and interests, their community involvement, the better able you are to respond to their needs.

- Wander around the plant or office daily. Stop by people's work areas to say "Hi."

- If your office has a door, leave it open. Closed doors send a signal that you don't want to interact with others; they breed distrust and suspicion. When you have private matters to discuss, adjourn to a conference room.

- Admit your mistakes. Be willing to say, "I don't know." Show that you're willing to change your mind when someone comes up with a better idea.

- Substantially increase people's signature authority. When people are entrusted to spend the organization's money responsibly, they feel more in control of their own work lives.

- Remove unnecessary steps in the approval processes for project proposals, change initiatives, or purchase of equipment. We've never seen an approval process that couldn't be shortened.

- On a weekly basis, share information about how your unit is doing in terms of meeting its goals. People want to know how things are going. This information makes them feel more powerful.

- When something needs to be done, ask for volunteers. When you give people a choice about being a part of what's happening, they're much more likely to be committed to a project.

- Publicize your team members' work. Every day, or at least every week, shine the spotlight on at least one person. At staff meetings, tell stories about people on the team or in another part of the organization who behaved in a way that truly exemplified what teamwork is all about.

- People get things done through a network of colleagues, not just up and down the hierarchy. Make sure you're connected to the key people in every part of the organization who are critical to your mission. Equally important, introduce your team members to the folks they need to know to get their jobs done.

- Make decisions visible. Use a centrally located bulletin board to post reminders of the team's decisions. Keep the board updated with information on progress toward goals.

- At least once a year, meet for an hour one-on-one with each of your direct reports or project team members. Talk about what motivates them, why they joined the organization, what they need to do their job the best they can, and their ideas for improvement. Make sure you act on what you learn.

- Conduct some of the training classes in your organization. By doing this you'll learn more about what it takes to teach a group, and you will also be able to develop the skill of developing others, which is essential to leadership.

- Volunteer to coach someone in a skill that you have. This coaching can be related to work or to an outside interest. The important thing is to hone your coaching skills so you can help others to improve.

- The time devoted to training in the average U.S. company is less than thirty hours per employee per year. The average for the best companies is closer to fifty hours per employee per year. Make sure that all the members of your group devote at least that much time to their individual development. Set the example by devoting fifty hours per year or more to your own learning.

- What else could you do to enhance people's sense of contribution and self-worth?

_____

_____

_____

- What else could you do to make people feel more in control of their own lives?

_____

_____

_____

- What else could you do to develop cooperative relationships with your team members or with colleagues in other units?

_____

_____

_____

- What else could you do to make yourself more accessible and open to others?

_____

_____

_____

_____

Learning from Others

- Hire a professional group facilitator to run several of your meetings. Carefully observe how the facilitator manages the group, encourages participation, and guides the group through the decision-making process.

- Try being a facilitator instead of a manager of meetings.

- Hire a personal coach to help you improve in a leadership practice or a sport. Notice the techniques this person uses and try out some of them when you are coaching your team members.

- Interview the coach of a professional or amateur athletic team in your area about what he or she does to help the team members perform at their best. Think about how you might apply the coach's methods in your organization.

- Choose someone in your organization who's known as an exceptional "people person." Accompany and observe this person for a few hours. Ask for tips on how you can improve the way you work with others.

- Ask someone you trust to observe the way you run a team meeting and work with your team members on a daily basis. Then ask the person to share his or her observations with you.

- Periodically trade places with employees and do their jobs. This is a terrific way to develop empathy and understanding, which contribute to trust.

- What else could you do to learn by example in Enable Others to Act?

_____

_____

_____

Learning in the Classroom or on Your Own

- Take a course in team building.

- Take a course in listening skills.

- Take a course in negotiation.

- Take a course on how to run meetings.

- Take a course on consulting skills.

- Take a course on performance management.

- Watch some videos on coaching.

- Read a book by a respected professional coach.

- Get on the Internet and join a chat room where people share effective ways of helping others achieve their best performance.

- Try out some groupware that helps foster collaboration, such as Lotus Notes® or Novell® GroupWise™.

- Study a social movement (for example, civil rights or women's suffrage) and find out how proponents encouraged others to become involved.

- What other courses, self-directed learning programs, or educational activities could you use to improve in Enable Others to Act?

_____

_____

_____

_____

Improving in Encourage The Heart

Getting extraordinary things done in organizations is hard work. Leaders recognize people's contributions and celebrate their accomplishments. They make people feel like heroes. Here are actions you can take to improve in Encourage the Heart.

Learning by Doing

- Say "thank you" when you appreciate something that someone has done.

- Wander around your office area for the express purpose of finding someone in the act of doing something that exemplifies the organization's standards. Find a way to recognize that person on the spot. For example, if you see someone who's voluntarily pitched in to coach a co-worker on how to use new software, tell the person how much you appreciate his or her efforts: "I really appreciate how you exemplify our value of teamwork. This is what it's all about."

- Think of three ways to single out (praise and reward) a constituent who best embodies the team's values and priorities. Use your imagination and have some fun. Give a giant light bulb to the person who has the best idea of the month or a box of candy to the person who makes the office run "sweetly." Give a penny to the person who takes a small step in improving his or the group's performance, a toy giraffe to the person who stuck her neck out to offer a suggestion. Have a "This Is Your Life" celebration for the person who has reached a milestone in tenure/commitment and have friends call in to say how that person made a difference.

- If your organization gives annual bonuses, link a portion of the bonus to the extent to which people model the organization's values.

- Plan a festive celebration for each small milestone that your team reaches. Don't wait until the whole project is finished to celebrate. Take the team out to lunch or take the afternoon off and go to a movie matinee. Have a picnic in the park with team members and their families. Put up a simple putt-putt golf game in the office hallway. Send around an ice cream cart to everyone's desk. A simple, fun celebration can break up the stress of an intense project.

- Look for opportunities to tell public stories about people in your organization who went above and beyond the call of duty.

- Instead of creating your reward and recognition systems yourself and imposing them on others, involve the key stakeholders—your direct reports, key peers, human resource professionals, or your manager. The resulting systems are more likely to link rewards to performance.

- Create a culture in which peers recognize peers. Give people tools that they can use to recognize one another's accomplishments and show their appreciation, such as index cards or notepads printed with the message "You Made My Day."

- Write at least three thank-you notes each day. We've never heard anyone complain about being thanked too much, but we've heard lots of complaints about being thanked too little!

- Put up a "bragging board" in a central place so that people can write public notes of thanks to colleagues who've done something to contribute to the values and victories of the team.

Encourage them to include bragging about their own accomplishments.

- Provide people with feedback about their results, and the sooner the better. Feedback can range from a simple "Well done" to a detailed debriefing session on how the latest project went and what the team members learned.

- Be personally involved. Not attending staff celebrations and parties sends the message that you're not interested.

- Set aside one day each year as a special organizational celebration day, much like Independence Day or Mardi Gras.

- Create your organization's "Hall of Fame"—an area that recognizes the people who've done extraordinary things.

- Put on a clown costume or other funny outfit and walk around the office distributing balloons. This may sound silly, but it will be noticed, you'll have fun, and it will liven up the place.

- What else can you do to recognize and reward individual contributions?

_____

_____

_____

_____

_____

_____

- What else can you do to celebrate team accomplishments?

_____

_____

_____

_____

_____

_____

Learning from Others

- Attend a high school football, soccer, or basketball game. Watch the cheerleaders and the players as they celebrate small wins and big victories. In your journal, note what you learned from your observations about their enthusiasm and passion.

- Ask for advice and coaching from someone who is much better at Encouraging the Heart than you are.

- Ask a variety of people how they like to be recognized for their accomplishments or successes.

- Attend an award ceremony for someone in your community or organization. In your journal, note what you liked about the ceremony, and try some of the same methods with an award ceremony for your own constituents.

- Whenever you attend a wedding or holiday celebration, record what you like about it and look for opportunities to use those ideas.

- Interview people in your organization who have a reputation for helping others to develop. Ask them how they encourage others to excel.

- What else could you do to learn from others to improve in Encourage the Heart?

_____

_____

_____

_____

_____

_____

_____

_____

_____

Learning in the Classroom or on Your Own

- Take an improvisational-theater class to help you become more comfortable with spontaneity.

- Take a class on creativity to help you find more creative ways of rewarding people.

- Take a course in drawing, painting, or photography so you can learn to be more expressive in the arts—a lot of reward and recognition is about expression.

- Take an advertising course so you can learn to write short messages that make the point and connect benefit (value) with what the person does.

- Take a class in story-telling.

- Take courses to learn what motivates people to achieve their best performance.

- What other courses, self-learning programs, and other activities would help you learn how to Encourage the Heart?

_____

_____

_____

_____

_____

_____

_____

_____

_____

_____

_____

RESOURCE C

Reading List

General Leadership

Warren Bennis, *On Becoming a Leader*. Reading, MA: Perseus, 1994.

MacGregor Burns, *Leadership*. New York: HarperCollins, 1978.

Jim Collins, *Good to Great: Why Some Companies Make the Leap and Others Don't*. New York: HarperCollins, 2001.

Jim Collins and Jerry Porras, *Built to Last: Successful Habits of Visionary Companies*. New York: HarperBusiness, 1994.

Howard Gardner, *Leading Minds: An Anatomy of Leadership*. New York: Basic Books, 1995.

John Gardner, *On Leadership*. New York: The Free Press, 1990.

James M. Kouzes and Barry Z. Posner, *The Leadership Challenge* (3rd ed.). San Francisco: Jossey-Bass, 2002.

James M. Kouzes and Barry Z. Posner, *Credibility: How Leaders Gain and Lose It, Why People Demand It* (2nd ed.). San Francisco: Jossey-Bass, 2003.

Tom Peters, *Liberation Management: Necessary Disorganization for the Nanosecond Nineties*. New York: Knopf, 1992.

Edgar H. Schein, *Organizational Culture and Leadership* (2nd ed.). San Francisco: Jossey-Bass, 1992.

Model the Way

David M. Armstrong, *Managing by Storying Around: A New Method of Leadership*. New York: Doubleday, 1992.

Peter Block, *The Answer to How Is Yes: Acting on What Matters*. San Francisco: Berrett-Koehler, 2002.

Steven R. Covey, *The Seven Habits of Highly Effective People*. New York: Simon & Schuster, 1989.

Max De Pree, *Leadership Is an Art*. New York: Doubleday, 1989.

Robert K. Greenleaf, *Servant Leadership: A Journey into Legitimate Power and Greatness*. Paulist Press, 1983.

David H. Maister. *Practice What You Preach: What Managers Must Do to Create a High Achievement Culture*. New York: The Free Press, 2001.

Parker J. Palmer, *Let Your Life Speak: Listening to the Voice of Vocation*. San Francisco: Jossey-Bass, 2000.

Terry Pearce, *Leading Out Loud: The Authentic Speaker, The Credible Leader*. San Francisco: Jossey-Bass, 1995.

Inspire a Shared Vision

Warren Bennis, Gretchen M. Spreitzer, and Thomas G. Cummings (Eds.), *The Future of Leadership: Today's Top Leadership Thinkers Speak to Tomorrow's Leaders*. San Francisco: Jossey-Bass, 2001.

Boyd Clarke and Ron Crossland, *The Leader's Voice: How Your Communication Can Inspire Action and Get Results!* New York: Select Books, 2002.

Gary Hamel, *Leading the Revolution*. Boston, MA: Harvard Business School Press, 2000.

Jennifer James, *Thinking in the Future Tense: Leadership Skills for the New Age*. New York: Simon & Schuster, 1996.

Burt Nanus, *Visionary Leadership*. San Francisco: Jossey-Bass, 1992.

Peter Schwartz, *The Art of the Long View*. New York: Currency/Doubleday, 1991.

Margaret Wheatley, *Leadership and the New Science*. San Francisco: Berrett-Koehler, 1992.

Challenge the Process

Arlene Blum, *Annapurna: A Woman's Place* (20th Anniversary Ed.). San Francisco: Sierra Club Books, 1998.

Mihaly Csikszentmihalyi, *Finding Flow: The Psychology of Engagement with Everyday Life*. New York: Basic Books, 1997.

Richard Farson and Ralph Keyes, *Whoever Makes the Most Mistakes Wins: The Paradox of Innovation*. New York: The Free Press, 2002.

Richard Foster and Sarah Kaplan, *Creative Destruction: Why Companies That Are Built to Last Underperform the Market—and How to Successfully Transform Them*. New York: Currency/Doubleday, 2001.

Ronald Heifitz and Marty Linsky, *Leadership on the Line: Staying Alive Through the Dangers of Leading*. Boston, MA: Harvard Business School Press, 2002.

Rosabeth Moss Kanter, Barry A. Stein, and T. D. Jick, *The Challenge of Organizational Change: How Companies Experience It and Leaders Guide It*. New York: The Free Press, 1992.

Tom Kelley with Jonathon Littman, *The Art of Innovation: Lessons in Creativity from IDEO, America's Leading Design Firm*. New York: Currency/Doubleday, 2001.

Robert J. Kriegel and Louis Patler, *If It Ain't Broke, Break It!* New York: Warner Books, 1991.

Enable Others to Act

D. Michael Abrashoff, *It's Your Ship: Management Techniques from the Best Damn Ship in the Navy*. New York: Warner, 2002.

Warren Bennis and Patricia Ward Biederman, *Organizing Genius: The Secrets of Creative Collaboration*. Reading, MA: Addison-Wesley, 1997.

Ken Blanchard, John Carlos, and Alan Randolph, *The Three Keys to Empowerment*. San Francisco: Berrett-Koehler, 1999.

Peter Block, *The Empowered Manager: Positive Political Skills at Work*. San Francisco: Jossey-Bass, 1987.

Marcus Buckingham and Curt Coffman, *First, Break All the Rules: What the World's Greatest Managers Do Differently*. New York: Simon & Schuster, 1999.

Cary Cherniss and Daniel Goleman (Eds.), *The Emotionally Intelligent Workplace: How to Select for, Measure, and Improve Emotional Intelligence in Individuals, Groups, and Organizations*. San Francisco: Jossey-Bass, 2001.

Robert B. Cialdini, *Influence: How and Why People Agree to Things*. New York: Morrow, 1984.

Roger Fisher and William Ury, *Getting to Yes*. New York: Penguin, 1988.

Daniel Goleman, *Working with Emotional Intelligence*. New York: Bantam, 1998.

Malcolm Gladwell, *The Tipping Point: How Little Things Make a Big Difference*. Boston, MA: Little, Brown and Company, 2002.

Charles A. O'Reilly and Jeffrey Pfeffer, *Hidden Value: How Great Companies Achieve Extraordinary Results with Ordinary People*. Boston, MA: Harvard Business School Press, 2000.

Jack Stack and Bo Burlingham, *A Stake in the Outcome: Building a Culture of Ownership for the Long-Term Success of Your Business*. New York: Currency/Doubleday, 2002.

Encourage the Heart

Ken Blanchard and Sheldon Bowles, *Gung Ho! Turn on the People in Any Organization*. New York: William Morrow, 1997.

Nathen Branden, *The Six Pillars of Self-Esteem*. New York: Bantam Books, 1994.

Terrence Deal and M. K. Deal, *Corporate Celebrations: Play, Purpose, and Profit at Work*. San Francisco: Berrett-Koehler, 1998.

Dave Hemsath and Leslie Yerkes, *301 Ways to Have Fun at Work*. San Francisco: Berrett-Koehler, 1997.

James M. Kouzes and Barry Z. Posner, *Encouraging the Heart: A Leader's Guide to Rewarding and Recognizing Others*. San Francisco: Jossey-Bass, 2003.

Ellen J. Langer, *Mindfulness*. Reading, MA.: Addison-Wesley, 1989.

Bob Nelson, *1001 Ways to Reward Employees*. New York: Workman, 1994.

Leadership Development

Ram Charan, Steve Drotter, and Jim Noel, *The Leadership Pipeline: How to Build the Leadership Powered Company*. San Francisco: Jossey-Bass, 2001.

Jay Conger and Beth Benjamin, *Building Leaders: How Successful Companies Develop the Next Generation of Leaders*. San Francisco: Jossey-Bass, 1999.

Daniel Goleman, Richard Boyatzis, and Annie McKee, *Primal Leadership: Realizing the Power of Emotional Intelligence*. Boston, MA: Harvard Business School Press, 2002.

John P. Kotter and Dan S. Cohen, *The Heart of Change: Real Life Stories of How People Change*. Boston, MA: Harvard Business School Press, 2002.

Morgan McCall, *High Flyers: Developing the Next Generation of Leaders*. Boston, MA: Harvard Business School Press, 1998.

Peter Senge et al. (Eds.), *Fifth Discipline Fieldbook: Strategies and Tools for Building a Learning Organization.* New York: Currency/Doubleday, 1994.

Mary K. Schwartz (Ed.), *Leadership Resources: A Guide to Training and Development Tools (8th ed.).* Greensboro, NC: Center for Creative Leadership, 2000.

Noel Tichy with Eli Cohen, *The Leadership Engine: How Winning Companies Build Leaders at Every Level.* New York: HarperCollins, 1997.

RESOURCE D

LEADERSHIP DEVELOPMENT WORKSHEET

Today's Date: _____

Leadership Development Period from _____ **to** _____

Leadership Practice Focus: _____

Leadership Behavior Focus: _____

Measurements of Progress:
Turn your ideal image into
measurable goals

_____

_____

_____

_____

_____

_____

_____

_____

_____

Primary Development Strategy:

Circle one primary strategy from among these three basic approaches to learning and development:

• Experience

• Example

• Education

Action Steps:

Using your primary strategy, what actions do you need to take to achieve your ideal image—your measurable goals?

_____

_____

_____

_____

_____

_____

_____

_____

_____

_____

_____

_____

_____

_____

_____

_____

Secondary Developmental Strategy:

Circle a secondary strategy

- **Experience**

- **Example**

- **Education**

Action Steps:

_____

_____

_____

_____

_____

_____

_____

_____

_____

_____

LEADERSHIP DEVELOPMENT WORKSHEET

Today's Date: _____

Leadership Development Period from _____ **to** _____

Leadership Practice Focus: _____

Leadership Behavior Focus: _____

Measurements of Progress:
Turn your ideal image into
measurable goals

_____

_____

_____

_____

_____

_____

_____

_____

_____

_____

**Primary Development
Strategy:**

Circle one primary strategy
from among these three
basic approaches to
learning and development:

• Experience

• Example

• Education

Action Steps:

Using your primary strategy, what actions
do you need to take to achieve your ideal
image—your measurable goals?

_____

_____

_____

_____

_____

_____

_____

_____

_____

_____

_____

_____

_____

_____

_____

Secondary Developmental Strategy:

Circle a secondary strategy

- **Experience**

- **Example**

- **Education**

Action Steps:

_____

_____

_____

_____

_____

_____

_____

_____

_____

Perhaps NONE OF us knows OUR *true* **strength** UNTIL challenged TO **bring** *it* forth.

ABOUT THE AUTHORS

Jim Kouzes is chairman emeritus of the Tom Peters Company, a professional services firm which inspires organizations to invent the new world of work using leadership training and consulting solutions. He is also an Executive Fellow at the Center for Innovation and Entrepreneurship at the Leavey School of Business, Santa Clara University. **Barry Posner** is Dean of The Leavey School of Business and Professor of Leadership at Santa Clara University (Silicon Valley, California), where he has received numerous teaching and innovation awards, including his school's and his university's highest faculty awards. Jim and Barry were named by the International Management Council as the 2001 recipients of the prestigious Wilbur M. McFeely Award. This honor puts them in the company of Ken Blanchard, Stephen Covey, Peter Drucker, Edward Deming, Francis Hesselbein, Lee Iacocca, Rosabeth Moss Kanter, Norman Vincent Peale, and Tom Peters, previous recipients of the award.

In addition to their award-winning and best-selling book, *The Leadership Challenge: How to Keep Getting Extraordinary Things Done in Organizations,* Jim and Barry have co-authored *Credibility: How Leaders Gain It and Lose It, Why People Demand It* (2003), chosen by *Industry Week* as one of that year's five best management books, *Encouraging the Heart* (2003) and *The Leadership Challenge Planner* (1999). Jim and Barry also developed the highly acclaimed *Leadership Practices Inventory* (LPI), a 360-degree questionnaire assessing leadership behavior; the LPI is one of the most widely used leadership assessment instruments in the world. More than 150 doctoral dissertations and academic research projects have been based on the *Five Practices of Exemplary Leadership*™ model. CRM Learning has produced a number of leadership and management development videos based upon their publications.

Jim and Barry are frequent conference speakers and each has conducted leadership development programs for hundreds of organizations including: Alcoa, Applied Materials, ARCO, AT&T, Australia Post, Bank of America, Bose, Charles Schwab, Cisco Systems, Conference Board of Canada, Consumers Energy, Dell Computer, Deloitte Touche, Egon Zehnder International, Federal Express, Gymboree, Hewlett-Packard, IBM, Johnson & Johnson, Kaiser Foundation Health Plans and Hospitals, Lawrence Livermore

National Labs, Leadership Greater Hartford, Levi Strauss & Co., L. L. Bean, 3M, Merck, Mervyn's, Motorola, Network Appliance, Pacific Telesis, Roche Bioscience, Siemens, Sun Microsystems, TRW, Toyota, US Postal Service, United Way, and VISA.

Jim Kouzes is featured as one of workplace experts in George Dixon's book, *What Works at Work: Lessons from the Masters* (1988) and *in Learning Journeys: Top Management Experts Share Hard-Earned Lessons on Becoming Great Mentors and Leaders,* edited by Marshall Goldsmith, Beverly Kaye, and Ken Shelton (2000). Not only is he a highly regarded leadership scholar and an experienced executive, but *The Wall Street Journal* has cited him as one of the twelve most requested non-university executive education providers to U.S. companies. A popular seminar and conference speaker, Jim shares his insights about the leadership practices that contribute to high performance in individuals and organizations, and he leaves his audiences inspired with practical leadership tools and tips that they can apply at work, at home, and in their communities.

Jim directed the Executive Development Center (EDC) at Santa Clara University from 1981 through 1987. Under his leadership the EDC was awarded two gold medals from the Council for the Advancement and Support of Education. He also founded the Joint Center for Human Services Development at San Jose State University, which he managed from 1972 until 1980, and prior to that was on the staff of the University of Texas School of Social Work. His career in training and development began in 1969 when Jim, as part of the Southwest urban team, conducted seminars for Community Action Agency staff and volunteers in the "war on poverty" effort. Jim received his B. A. degree (1967) with honors from Michigan State University in political science and a certificate (1974) from San Jose State University's School of Business for completion of the internship in organization development.

Jim's interest in leadership began while he was growing up in Washington, D.C. In 1961 he was one of a dozen Eagle Scouts selected to serve in John F. Kennedy's Honor Guard at the presidential inauguration. Inspired by Kennedy, he served as a Peace Corps volunteer from 1967 through 1969. Jim can be reached at 408-978-1809 or jim@kouzesposner.com.

Barry Posner, an internationally renowned scholar and educator, is the author or coauthor of more than a hundred research and practitioner-focused articles in such publications as *Academy of Management Journal, Journal of Applied Psychology, Human Relations, Personnel Psychology, IEEE Transaction on Engineering Management, Journal of Business Ethics, California Management Review, Business Horizons,* and *Management Review.* In addition to his books with Jim Kouzes, he has coauthored several books on project management, most recently *Checkered Flag Projects: Ten Rules for Creating and Managing Projects That Win!* Barry is on the editorial review boards for the *Journal of Management Inquiry* and *Journal of Business Ethics.*

Barry received his B. A. degree (1970) with honors from the University of California, Santa Barbara, in political science. He received his M. A. degree (1972) from The Ohio State University in public administration and his Ph.D. degree (1976) from the

University of Massachusetts, Amherst, in organizational behavior and administrative theory. Having consulted with a wide variety of public and private sector organizations around the globe, Barry currently sits on the Board of Directors for the American Institute of Architects (AIA). He served previously on the boards of Public Allies, Big Brothers/Big Sisters of Santa Clara County, the Center for Excellence in Non-Profits, Sigma Phi Epsilon Fraternity, and several start-up companies. At Santa Clara University he has previously served as Associate Dean for Graduate Programs and Managing Partner for the Executive Development Center.

Barry's interest in leadership began as a student during the turbulent unrest on college campuses in the late 1960s, when he was participating and reflecting on the balance between energetic collective action and chaotic and frustrated anarchy. At one time, he aspired to be a Supreme Court justice, but realizing he would have to study law, he redirected his energies into understanding people, organizational systems, and the liberation of the human spirit. Barry can be reached at (408) 554-4523 or bposner@scu.edu.

More information about Jim and Barry, and their work, can be found at their Web site: www.theleadershipchallenge.com.